Meditation

Guided Meditations And Comforting Bedtime Stories For Adults Who Are Struggling With Stress And Illness: You Are Really On A Path To Healing Right Now

(Techniques Of Quick Meditation To Get Rid Of Anxiety And Stress In Order To Experience Happiness)

Arno Egger

TABLE OF CONTENT

Introduction 1

The Seven Chakras 3

How To Free Your Body Of Its 7 Latent Energy Centers 13

The Phrase "Manipura" The Solar Chakra Is Also Known As The Solar Plexus. 22

What Are Chakras? 30

General Principles That Will Assist You In Determining Which Chakra To Awaken 37

Your Sacred Center When It Comes To Relationships 43

The Beauty Is In Achieving A Good Balance. ... 61

The Process Of Healing The Seventh Chakra ... 76

Meditations Using Chakra Mantras To Release Blocked Energy 90

Concerning The Area Of The Sacral Chakra 95

The Heart Chakra 116

The Practices Of Yoga And Traditional Chinese Medicine 124

The Base Chakra 135
Bringing Back The Sense Of Balance To The Heart Chakra 147
Bringing Our Life Force Into Harmony And Purification... 165

Introduction

In the subtle body, there are points of energy known as chakras. A physical body is not equivalent to a subtle body in any way. Every subtle body is connected in some way to a hierarchy, which is also frequently referred to as a vast chain of being, and this hierarchy will ultimately arrive at its pinnacle of growth somewhere inside the physical world. Every subtle body also has a corresponding subtle realm, which may be thought of as just an additional dimension or level of existence. A subtle body may be conceptualized in the same way as a soul or an orb, depending on your point of view. They do not exist (or live) in the same physical world that our physical bodies do; hence, in order for them to continue living, it is necessary for them to have their own physical reality.

The function of a chakra is to bring together a number of different energy pathways. These energy pathways are also known by the term "nadi." It is a central tenet of many Indian religious traditions that the Nadi are the conduits inside the subtle body through which the para, which refers to the non-physical energy that flows through us and is also known as vital energy. The chakras are the points where all of this energy converges. According to the teachings of these Indian faiths, there are a total of seven chakras, and each of them has the ability to influence not only the mind but also the body and spirit in a variety of distinct ways.

The Seven Chakras

There are hundreds of points in your body at which energy may be directed and concentrated. Chakras, on the other hand, are the names given to the seven primary locations at which the primary energy centers are situated. Every portion of your body is adequately represented along the chakra route, which runs from the base of your spine to the crown of your head. The seven chakras in your body are distributed between these two points. Each of the chakras in your body relates to a different facet of your awareness and carries out a unique set of tasks. The chakras are responsible for the flow of energy from the crown of the head all the way down to the base of the spine.

In addition, each chakra has a particular gland within the endocrine system of the body that it is associated with, as well as a hue that falls somewhere on the spectrum of the rainbow. On some level—emotional, mental, physical, or spiritual—the knowledge contained in each hue may be accessed. This knowledge is often used in the process of chakra healing and balancing via the utilization of a technique known as color healing; we will discuss this later on in the lesson.

An illustration of the seven primary chakras and their associated auric fields is shown below.

1. The Chakra of the Root (Base)

This energy point, known as the chakra, is the first of the seven. It may be found near the bottom of the spine, just slightly above the genital region, and the color red that corresponds to it in the rainbow spectrum describes its appearance. The base of the spine, the feet, the rectum, the legs, the bones, the sexual organs, the immune system, the pelvis, the appendix, the bladder, and the hips are all related with the root chakra. Additionally, it is connected to the concepts of rooted, supporting, and anchoring.

A person's levels of physical vitality and their desire to exist in the physical world are also related with the base chakra, in addition to their interconnection with previous lifetimes and the earth. The base chakra is located at the tailbone. Before your energy may access the higher chakra centers, it must first be transmuted and refined by this chakra. This is the primary function of this chakra.

This chakra is where sexually inspired energy is generally held, and you can always activate it via yoga to cause it to ascend through each of the other chakras and all the way up to the crown chakra. Your knowledge and spiritual development of other levels of energy will increase as you continue to practice this.

You'll have a strong desire to life, and you'll be brimming with physical vitality, if you keep your root chakra open and make sure it's functioning properly. Your physical vitality is cut off when it is weak or obstructed, and you are unable to make a powerful physical impression when this occurs.

In the event that your root chakra is underdeveloped, you will experience a loss of both physical strength and coordination. You will notice that you avoid engaging in any kind of physical activity, and it will be difficult for you to physically express yourself. If your root chakra is weak, you may also get the sensation of not being grounded and of lacking a solid basis.

If it reaches to the point where it is too reactive, you will never be able to be happy with simply being in one location, and you will be seeking for something to do or somewhere else to go all the time. If your root chakra is open but not working properly, you may have a predisposition toward aggressive behavior in the physical world.

This chakra is related with a number of different bodily ailments, such as persistent lower back pain, stress in the spine, constipation, pelvic discomfort, sexual potency issues, urinary difficulties, colon cancer, and so on. Insecurities, aggressive behavior, gluttony, and resentment are some of the other issues that are linked to the root chakra.

Meditation on the Heart Chakra 2

Place yourself on a level surface and lie down. Check that you are not experiencing any discomfort. Put a stop to your yawning.

Take a long, deep inhale, and then gently let the air out of your lungs. Repeat this action a further two times.

After that, take a deep breath in and then wrap your arms around your body as if you were hugging yourself. In addition, when you exhale, bring your arms down to your sides and let them relax on the ground in front of you.

While you are lying on your back, let yourself to experience both the vulnerability you feel as a person as well as the connection you feel to the land.

Stay as calm as possible and take a couple more deep breaths, making sure to exhale gently each time.

Close your eyes and imagine that when you exhale, you are letting go of all of the bad energy that have been weighing you down.

Every time you let out an exhale, give yourself permission to release all of the negative energy that are holding you back, such as avarice, wrath, hatred, and envy.

And as you draw in air, picture good and fresh life energy streaming through your whole body.Do this as you inhale.

Pay attention to the cadence of your own breathing. The sound you hear is the rhythm of your heart pounding. Each and every beat is important because it brings fresh energy into your body. Every time your heart beats, you should be reminding yourself that you have the capacity to both give and receive love.

Relax both your physical self and your mental self.

The next time you take a breath in, let the love that is freely flowing all around you to enter your heart as you do so.

Send forth the love that you have and feel for the people around you as you let the breath out of your body.

Permit the feeling of love to permeate your whole body.

Stay lying down for the next several minutes. Take use of this opportunity to rid your heart of all feelings of fear, rage, hatred, jealousy, and resentment.

Now, when you are ready, gently open your eyes, and share the love that you feel with your family, friends, and that one person who really stands out to you.

You should share the love that is in your heart with other people, as well as be open to receiving any love that is sent in your direction.

How To Free Your Body Of Its 7 Latent Energy Centers

You may not be aware of it, but instead, everyone of us individually have an energy field that permeates our bodies and is segmented into numerous zones. You might not know about it. The seven chakras are the actual energy centers, and they are the ones that are most well recognized. Your life will be filled with greater exhilaration, creativity, and joy if you open these seven energy focuses.

This electromagnetic energy field, which is also referred to as an emanation, is not visible to the naked eye since it is an emission. Even if it's possible that you didn't see it, you definitely would have felt it in the end. For instance, have you ever dedicated your time and effort with someone who had a pessimistic viewpoint? This person maintained control of the conversation, and the primary focus of the conversation was on the many aspects of this person's life that were problematic at the moment. At the end of the visit, your friend will thank you and remark that having a conversation with you has made a significant improvement in how they feel, but you will leave the visit feeling emotionally drained.

Because they have strengthened their own energy field while depleting yours, they are able to feel better as a result. You will have the ability to manage the potent energy of your seven energy foci and prevent this sort of depletion if you become a Reiki Master. This ability will come about as a result of your training to become a Reiki Master.

The following is a list of the seven energy foci that run down the spine:

the first Chakra may be located just below the tailbone.

the second Chakra is located near the base of the spine, in the space between the pelvic bones.

The third Chakra is located just below the navel.

the fourth Chakra, located right next to your heart

The fifth Chakra is located at the back of the throat.

sixth Chakra: located in the middle of the cerebrum

seventh Chakra — located straight above the head, on top of the crown

These energy centers, or chakras, are interconnected and exert influence on many parts of our anatomy.

When we think about reiki, we think of spiritual energy and in-depth healing, but in reality, it is a great deal more than that. Utilize Reiki to clear out any obstructions in your chakras and sufficiently energize them. This practice also has a wide variety of other applications, such as aiding in the discovery of your true purpose and the recovery from any previous injuries. After you have opened all of your chakras and restored your vital energy, you will notice that life takes on a new level of significance. You develop into a person who is more vivacious, kind, and appreciative of life, and this quality is reflected in your day-to-day activities, which cause you to think about the people in your immediate environment. Learning Reiki is an investment not just in your own well-being but also in the well-being of those closest to you, including your friends and loved ones. It's possible that you don't believe you have enough energy, but the truth is that you do. It is similar to anything else, you will need to dedicate some time to learning it, but thankfully, it is quick and easy to pick up.

Unlocking Your Psychic Capabilities

Everyone has a certain amount of mental strength. However, there are certain persons who have greater intellectual potential than others and possess more skills. Even though everyone has at least a small bit of supernatural energy, 99.9% of people do not open their power and allow it to go to waste. This is despite the fact that everyone possesses at least a little bit of supernatural energy. It's conceivable that they don't believe they have psychic ability, or that they aren't aware of how to tap into it. Both of these are possibilities. Make every effort to prevent it from coming to pass.

Open Your Mind to Psychic Capabilities

Discovering how to harness your psychic strength may improve your life by allowing you to make use of supernatural abilities such as clairvoyance, perceptiveness, astral travel, clear imagining, psychomancy, and clairsentience. You get the picture. Once you have access to your psychic powers, you will have the ability to quickly and easily learn how to utilize any one of the many skills that are available to you.

The Essential Blunder That Nearly All People Commit

The great majority of people, when they first start making an effort to develop their psychic potential, make the key error of not paying significant regard to the privilege chakras. This is the mistake that costs them the most ground. What exactly are the chakras? They are the points of concentration of energy in your brain and body that give you access to your intuitive faculties. They need to be set in stone and tweaked with the ultimate objective of making the most of your perceptive nature. The following are the three "super chakras" that are essential to the process of expanding your capabilities:

The Crown Chakra is in charge of connecting us with the overall energy supply that is all around us. It is situated at the very top of the head, and its location gives it this responsibility. This is the item that allows psychics to utilize their intuition to fuel their psychic skills. Psychics' talents are powered by their intuition.

The Brow Chakra is the chakra that is most often referred to as "the third eye."

It is responsible for linking the conscious mind with the deepest levels of the subconscious mind. In order for a psychic to make use of their skills, the Brow Chakra has to be relaxed and open.

This chakra is in charge of your psychic ability and intuition. It is located in the heart. Your natural intellectual capacity is located in the centre of the structure. By rerouting your intuitive energy from your heart chakra to your crown chakra, you may unlock the extraordinary power that lies dormant within you.

The Phrase "Manipura" The Solar Chakra Is Also Known As The Solar Plexus.

The quality of fire is referred to as the Manipura. It has something to do with one's perception of color and sight. This chakra may be discovered on the area of the umbilicus that corresponds to the stomach or the solar plexus. This chakra has an effect on a person's feeling of well-being, their capacity to comprehend and cope with emotional issues, their stamina, as well as their willpower and ego. When the manipura charka is out of balance, it may have a variety of negative effects. These conditions include diabetes, arthritis, stomach discomfort and ulcers, low blood pressure, low self-esteem, depression, inability to make choices, animosity, and bad decision making skills. Others include poor decision making abilities and poor decision making abilities. Anger and fits of wrath are also common experiences for certain individuals. When all of the chakras are functioning properly, not only is there an abundance of energy, but the individual also has the self-assurance and shrewdness necessary to make sound choices. When this chakra is in a state of healthy equilibrium, it makes it possible to have a positive mental concentration, excellent digestive health, and increased productivity throughout the day. Essential oils derived from herbs like rosemary and lavender are among those that are claimed to strengthen this chakra.

The Solar Plexus, also known as the Manipura Chakra, is the source of a variety of emotional issues, including poor self-esteem, a negative self-image, and a lack of vitality. It is also capable of causing rage, the need to prove one's superiority over others, and the obsession with attaining absolute perfection in all aspects of one's life. This may lead to the development of depression as well as a demand for stimulants in the individual. Participating in yoga practices such as the Half Boat Pose, Leg Lifts, and the Boat Pose are all excellent for balancing the third chakra, which is one of the most important chakras. Yoga is extremely helpful for this chakra.

This chakra, which may be found right above the navel, is responsible for the upper abdomen, the liver, the pancreas, the middle spine, the gall bladder, the adrenals, the kidney, the spleen, the stomach, and the small intestine.

Your self-confidence, development, capacity for self-control, sense of humor, self-power, ego power, and digestion are all influenced by the chakra. When this chakra is out of whack, it may lead to a number of health difficulties, including diabetes, constipation, digestive troubles, ulcers, issues with self-esteem, hypersensitivity to criticism, worries related to self-image, anxiousness, and poor memory.

Your sense of self-worth is governed by the Manipura chakra. Your solar plexus chakra is the source of your mental awareness, ego, optimism, willpower, and confidence. Your capacity to concentrate and your understanding of the world around you are both controlled by the energy center known as the chakra. This chakra is the conduit for the expression of your innate inclinations.

The Heart Chakra: The Ability to Love

The fourth chakra, also known as the heart chakra, is situated in the middle of the chest, directly above the heart. Its Sanskrit name is "Anahata," which translates as "unstruck" or "unhurt," and its location is directly above the heart. Both the respiratory and circulatory systems of the body are linked to it.

This chakra represents the force of love, and it is connected to the processes of healing and maintaining health. The element of air serves as its foundation. It is the link that binds the mind, the body, the soul, and the emotions all together. The love, beauty, compassion, kindness, empowerment, and connection that we experience in our lives come from the heart chakra.

This chakra's energy is related with expansiveness as well as a connection to everything in the universe. In spite of the fact that most people associate it with the color pink, its true meaning is really associated with the color green. The representation of a chakra consists of a circle with twelve petals, a triangle pointing downwards entwined with another triangle pointing upwards to form a six-pointed star or hexagram, and a triangle pointing upwards to complete the sign.

Put your sorrow at the forefront of your mind in order to restore harmony to the heart chakra. Spend some time giving your sentiments of loss and despair the respect and appreciation they deserve. This enlightens us to the fact that it is precisely the suffering that we experience in our lives that teaches us how to let go and forgive; when we are able to do so, we are in a position to love more deeply.

The Heart Chakra and Other Non-Traditional Methods of Healing

Green is the color.

Air, the element

Localization: in the middle of the chest, directly over the heart

Ailments of the Emotions Caused by Blockages: Behaviors such as being antisocial and feeling lonely, having poor boundaries, being codependent, and concentrating too much on other people

Asthma, respiratory issues, feeling weary or worn out, severe skin problems, susceptibility to colds and coronary or circulation disorders are some examples of the physical ailments that may result from blockages.

Rose Quartz, Tsavorite garnet, watermelon tourmaline, rainbow fluorite, pink topaz, peridot, moss agate, mangano calcite, malachite, labradorite, jade, green apatite, fuchsite, eudialyte, emerald, aventurine, amazonite, and alexandrite are some of the crystals that may be used for healing with crystals.

Lemon balm, thyme, white horn, and other medicinal herbs include: A. Melissa

The Bach Method of Healing Willow, red chestnut, and chicory flowers are used in flower therapy.

Jasmine, rose, tarragon, and vanilla essential oils have been shown to be therapeutic.

Using sound to heal, chant the "YAM" sound, which is the universal seed sound.

Using affirmations to facilitate healing: "My heart is open to love." "I accept myself with kindness and compassion." "I give and receive with a heart that is open to all living beings,"

Listen to music that you like, wear the color green, have a massage, hug and comfort other people, connect with nature, and spend time outdoors are all great ways to activate the heart chakra.

Meditation and Yoga Pose: Fish Pose or the Cobra Pose

What Are Chakras?

In India, there has been a well-developed tradition of studying the human body, as well as its vitality and potential, for thousands of years. Your body is made up of seven different centers, and those centers may be found dispersed all across the body. These centers form the body's energy foundation. You will be astounded at the effects that may be observed in both your day-to-day life and in all of the work that you do when you are able to align all of your energy centers. These results can be experienced in both areas simultaneously. Through the effective alignment of intent and purpose, you will have the ability to identify methods to concentrate your energy as well as to transcend your own obstacles to success in your pursuit of success.

A Brief Overview of Chakra History:

In the Western culture, the practice of meditation, as well as the tradition of really comprehending the requirements of the spiritual body, are relatively recent developments. Over 6,000 years ago in India, the tradition of Hinduism gave rise to yoga. Yoga was first practiced in India. It appears in the book as a reference to a means to be able to balance all of the energy in your body as well as a way to be able to connect with the universal energies that flow throughout the universe. Additionally, it refers to a technique to be able to connect with the energies that flow throughout the universe. It is believed that all of the energy in the cosmos may be tapped into via the body as it is transferred from one chakra to the next. This is something that has been passed down through traditions and teachings. The original meaning of the term yoga, which derives from Sanskrit, is "union." The word "wheel" is where the term "chakra" originates from. This signified that all of the body's energies were constantly moving in a circular motion throughout the body, making it possible to channel all of these energies at the same time, allowing for the transmission of energy from one part of the body to another, as well as the concentration and channeling of energy for any purpose that may be necessary. Chakras can be found throughout the body.

According to the teachings of yoga, it is possible to flow energy in any direction and from one spot to another. There are in fact seven chakras that may be aligned from the head to the foot. It is believed that the alignment of the chakras runs in a direct alignment to the seven stars that make up the Big Dipper, and that this alignment is also parallel to the stars in the night sky.

A portion of the human body that the Hindus have been aware of for more than 6,000 years and that is referred to as the subtle body is called the causal body. On top of this portion of the spirit, which is linked to the cosmos and serves as a support for the chakras, is the crown chakra. It is the means by which the physical body is able to concentrate on itself and by which it may connect with the energy of the cosmos. The subtle body is also known as the collective unconscious, the power of the mind to use the chakras to connect into the mind and the universe via its universal intelligence, and a condition of sleep or meditation. It is also possible to describe the subtle body as the power of the mind to use the chakras to plug into the mind and the universe.

In a manner quite similar to that of the Romans, the Hindus were aware that to be animated meant that your soul included breath. The term "prana" refers to this kind of vitality in Hinduism. It was believed that pranatraveled through the subtle body as a stream travels through a field, carrying the energy and the liveliness from one chakra to the next in a manner that was analogous to the flow of water. This connection was what served to maintain the life of the person and enabled them to tap into the marvels of the cosmos that were around them. Both of these things were possible because of the person's ability to connect. People in Western cultures find it challenging to comprehend this idea since there is nothing comparable in the contemporary world that discusses the link that exists between the mind and the body. The vast majority of western religions and philosophical schools of thought focus only on the spirit, and they don't say much about the link between the two outside the fact that the body is the spirit's temple.

General Principles That Will Assist You In Determining Which Chakra To Awaken

1. Get Familiar with Your Chakras

Learning about your chakras is one of the most critical steps you can take in being ready to open them. Each of the chakras has a variety of distinctive traits that are unique from those possessed by the others. That also implies that the process of opening them is rather different from other doors. When our chakras are out of balance or blocked, we may experience feelings of disorientation or exhaustion. It's possible that we'll become sick, too. Learn what each chakra stands for as well as the symptoms that indicate they are either blocked or out of balance. This will allow you to properly care for them when the situation calls for it.

The second step is to determine the extent of the need.

Because you have a total of seven chakras, also known as energy centers, you need to figure out which one you want to work on first. It is not always easy to determine which of the individuals needs assistance more than the others. This is due to the fact that any one that is out of alignment has an effect on the others. There are a few indicators that you may check up to determine which chakra is causing you the most difficulty. One of the first things you should do is do the chakra test, which is examining every region of your body to determine which one has the most issues.

In addition, you should determine whether or not you are experiencing any kind of bodily discomfort in the place that corresponds to the chakra that is being referred to. You may also evaluate what is going on in your life and discover significant concerns, such as money difficulties, safety issues, marital troubles, an emotional roller coaster, or a lack of drive, among other things. There is also the option of consulting the services of a professional who specializes in chakra energy healing, as well as a close friend or colleague who is energy-conscious.

Activate the Energy to Open Your Chakras, which Is the Third Step

You should now be able to identify the chakra that is causing you trouble. Now is the time to start making a plan for how to open that chakra, and it is essential that you also consider this to be a strategy for restoring your chakra. When you open this chakra, you are not only harmonizing the flow of your energy (both intake and outflow), but you are also expanding your awareness of the state that it may take and the ways in which it can change. The notion of balancing or achieving equilibrium while opening your chakras is the primary concept that is used by both trained healers and the majority of individuals who are energy sensitive.

During the process of opening your chakra, you will need to engage in a variety of practices, such as exercises that concentrate on your breathing and physical activities in which you direct your attention to a specific area of your body. Participate in a healing session (you may do this by finding a professional healer or an energy-conscious individual), employ chakra connection methods or massages (also known as "self-healing hands-on technique"), and practice a meditation technique that focuses on that specific chakra area.

It is important that you keep in mind that other things may present themselves throughout the process of attempting to restore your chakra using any one of these several ways. When you are working to open your chakras, it is important to keep in mind the factors that caused them to become blocked or out of balance in the first place. You should take advantage of this opportunity to proactively address these issues since they are more likely to arise in the future. Always remember to take care of yourself by making sure you are focused, attentive, and conscious of everything that is going on around you while you are opening your chakras.

When deciding which method is best for opening your chakras, it is important to first determine whatever practice speaks to you or makes the most intuitive sense. Consider whether or not you would benefit more from a contemplative or physical practice. You could just have a few minutes, but you might also be able to arrange an hour or more of practice time. Depending on your availability, the sort of exercise you choose will also be determined.

Your Sacred Center When It Comes To Relationships

Sometimes, maintaining healthy relationships might seem like an uphill battle. It is much too common for us to say things we later regret when we are frustrated, or to behave in unpleasant ways when we are angry. In unfortunate circumstances such as these, the Sacral shows to be of assistance. It is true that the energy of the sacral chakra is the source of our libido and intimate relationships, but it is also the source of our compassion and acceptance of others. When we allow ourselves to be guided by these aspects of the Sacral Chakra, we are able to navigate difficult confrontations with a great deal more success, and this is true regardless of whether or not these confrontations take place amongst friends, family members, spouses, or colleagues. In light of the aforementioned, give the following exercise a go the next time you find yourself in a heated discussion with someone you care about and need to keep your cool by biting your tongue:

You will need to put in some practice time before doing this exercise successfully. Don't let it get to you, however. This method is efficient and uncomplicated:

1. Devote a total of twenty minutes every week to serving as practice time.

2. Go to a place where you won't be disturbed and sit on the floor with your legs crossed.

3. Think back to a time in your life when you could have shown greater compassion and acceptance toward other people. Imagine the specifics of the predicament in your mind. Where were

you last night? Who were you with at that time? What did you have on your body? Where were you and what did you see? What have you been hearing? How did you experience it?

4. While you are doing this, put your hands on your hips and remain with them in that position for the whole twenty minute period. (The sacral region is represented by the hips, which are a component of the pelvic bone).

5. Regularly bring your attention to the fact that your hands are resting on your hips. After sufficient repetition, you'll eventually come to equate the position of your hands on your hips with the need to be more tolerant and sympathetic.

When things become difficult, put your hands on your hips. (However, use extreme caution. (You shouldn't make this into a hostile or defensive motion.)

During difficult circumstances, all that is required of us at times is a simple reminder to have compassion and acceptance for those around us. If you have followed the steps stated above, the simple act of placing your hands for a little while on your hips should serve as a reminder of the need for you to be more welcoming and caring.

Vishuddha, the throat chakra, is where speech is generated.

Located near the neck; its color is light blue; its element is space; and the word associated with it is communication.

The Throat Chakra Will Be Unlocked When...

The following gemstones are considered to be crystals: turquoise, sodalite, aquamarine, blue agate, lapis lazuli, sapphire, and blue topaz

Bergamot, tea tree, and chamomile are some of the herbs and oils used.

Sound: Note G, frequency 384 Hz, birds singing and crickets chirping, bij mantra: Ham

Sea plants, soups, sauces, fruits that keep you hydrated, teas, a range of fruits and vegetables, currants, blackberries, blueberries, dragon fruit, kelp, kombu, barley, wheatgrass, and mushrooms are some examples of foods.

SalambaSarvangasana, Halasana, Matsyasana, and SetuBhandasana are some of the Yoga Poses.

Thyroid, neck, jaw, mouth, dental, communication, will, timing, integration, authenticity, harmony, choice, chewing, and expressing one's truth are some of the things this house rules.

"I am able to articulate my thoughts in a manner that is graceful and honest."

My throat chakra has always been the one that has been the most challenging for me to maintain open. It is imperative that I continue to work on it so that it does not become unusable again. In my family, thyroid problems run rampant, and I've struggled mightily with a number of neck issues over the years. However, this only addresses the purely physical aspects of the Throat chakra. There is also an emotional component, which consists of learning how to advocate for oneself and learning how to take ownership of one's own authenticity. You may shut this down by listening to the pessimistic discourse of everyone else. If this is the case, you are the one who is engaging in negative self-talk. Your Throat chakra will begin to constrict if you do not make an effort to articulate what is true to you. If your Throat chakra is blocked, it will be extremely difficult for you to interact with other people. When my throat chakra is entirely blocked, I find it far easier to isolate myself in the midst of a thick forest or up in the mountains than to engage in conversation with even a single person. If you are sick with a cold, a sore throat, or a sinus infection, give some thought to the truth that lies inside you.

It may be quite draining on the Throat chakra for persons whose jobs need them to engage with the general public on a regular basis. It is possible that your Throat chakra may shut up on you despite your best efforts to prevent it from happening no matter how hard you try to keep it open. After then, the only thing you can do is continue to work on unlocking it from that point on. Having a sore throat is often a warning indication that you are bottling up your feelings or failing to express yourself. This is due to an accumulation of bad energy that has been stuck in your Throat chakra.

Activating your Throat chakra may be accomplished most effectively by letting your soul be heard. This may be done in whatever manner of expression with which you are most at ease. Even while verbal exchange is the most effective method of communication, this is not always about words. Singing, drawing, typing, or any other method of expression that comes to mind are all forms of communication. This might even be documented in a personal diary. Communicate, communicate, and communicate some more!!!!!!!! Release whatever you've been harboring inside of you for so long. Give vent to the feelings that you have repressed for so long inside of you. Keep a diary if you are confident in your writing abilities so that you may record the thoughts and feelings that you are unable or unable to share with the rest of the world. You will be able to repair and unleash the potential of your Throat chakra so long as you release it and do not cling to it in any way. Crystals are also of great assistance in working with the Throat chakra. You may choose any or all of the crystals that are associated with the Throat chakra to make a necklace for yourself.

Producing any kind of music or noise might also be of assistance. It is not even necessary for them to be words. whatever it is that makes you feel the most at ease.

Crystals That Are Linked Together

Angelite, Blue Lace Agate, Chrysocolla, and Kyanite are some examples of gemstones.

Angelite is known as the stone of consciousness. It makes psychic communication easier to achieve. It encourages the body to mend itself. Speaking your truth might be beneficial to you. It is possible to make touch with the ethereal or angelic dimension via the use of this tool, as its name indicates. It deepens one's capacity for understanding, compassion, and acceptance. It makes for a more serene and peaceful environment.

Added Advantages

It reduces swelling and inflammation. It brings the thyroid and parathyroid glands back into equilibrium. It maintains a healthy equilibrium between the body's fluids. It does so via repairing blood vessels as well as tissue. It soothes the skin and helps prevent sunburn. It is possible to utilize it to maintain a healthy weight. The energy system and the meridians both become unblocked as a result of this.

Putting in place

You are free to either hold it or position it on the body as you see fit.

Safeguarding of

It provides protection not just to individuals but also to the natural world. It is a symbol of tranquility. It relieves the mental anguish caused by it. It is an effective means of combating harsh behavior. As a result of its ability to deepen attunement and heighten perception, it is an excellent stone for use by healers.

ORIGINAL SOURCE

Egypt, Mexico, Peru, Poland, Germany, Britain, and Libya are some of the countries included.

The healing of one's throat chakra is facilitated very well by blue lace agate, which also encourages the expression of one's ideas and emotions. It helps one to articulate the spiritual truth that is inside them. It establishes a connection between the ideas and the spiritual vibration. It creates an atmosphere that is calm and serene.

Added Advantages

It is highly efficient in treating infections of the throat, thyroid, and lymphatic system. It is helpful for alleviating issues with the neck and shoulders. Fractures are helped to mend, the skeletal system is strengthened, fevers are lowered, and the pancreas is supported by this. It is effective in the treatment of arthritis as well as bone deformities. It is possible to use it in the field of sound therapy. When ingested in the form of an elixir, it has the potential to correct imbalances in the brain.

Putting in place

Place specifically in the region of the neck, or wherever else that seems suitable.

Safeguarding of

It breaks down previous habits of repression and promotes expression, particularly in situations in which a person is afraid of being evaluated by others. It brings about a state of calm. It makes it easier for males to acknowledge and accept their emotions.

Morocco, Africa, India, Brazil, the United States of America, and the Czech Republic all served as sources.

Chrysocolla has the ability to purify, soothe, and revitalize all of the chakras. It eliminates any and all negative forms of energy. It encourages people to communicate. It heightens both one's awareness of oneself and one's inner equilibrium. It encourages honest conversation while also stimulating creative thought. It is a wonderful stone that may make one's life happier in many ways.

Added Advantages

Both the thyroid and the metabolism get benefits from this supplement. It brings the blood pressure down. It is beneficial for the healing of throat infections in addition to the tonsils. It purifies the kidneys, liver, and intestines, to name a few of the organs that benefit from this process. It restores equilibrium to the circulation, supplies oxygen to the blood, and aids in the development of the cellular structure of the lungs. As a result, it makes breathing easier. It does this while also regulating insulin levels in the body and regenerating the pancreas. It helps to prevent muscular spasms and makes existing ones easier to bear. It alleviates the painful symptoms of PMS and menstruation.

Putting in place

You are free to position it anywhere you see fit on the body.

Safeguarding of

When it is brought into the house, it eliminates any bad energy that may be there. It contributes to the stabilization of relationships that have been troubled. It helps one accept change and lowers the mental tension that comes with adapting to new situations. It also stimulates the development of one's inner power. It is beneficial in overcoming phobias and promotes increased self-awareness.

Mexico, Zaire, Peru, Chile, Russia, the United States of America, and Britain are all sources.

The spiritual energy is brought down to earth through kyanite. It brings alignment to the chakras as well as the subtle bodies. Since it does not harbor any bad energy, it does not need any kind of purification. It inspires one to communicate what they know to be true. It is beneficial to meditation. It fosters intuitive thinking and enhances psychic powers. Stress, anger, frustration, and obstructions are all released as a result. It helps one remember their dreams. It teaches one to have compassion. Attunements may be performed quite well with this gem.

Added Advantages

It is a pain reliever. It leads to a reduction in blood pressure. It brings the yin and the yang energies into harmony. It is beneficial in the treatment of infections. It is helpful in reducing overall body fat. The urogenital system, the thyroid, the parathyroid, the throat, and the adrenal glands are some of the body parts that may be treated with it. It brings down temperature and is helpful when taken for diseases that affect the muscles.

Putting in place

You may either hang it around your neck like a necklace or position it in the space between your navel and your heart. You may put it on any part of your body that is hurting you and it will help.

Brazil is the original.

The Beauty Is In Achieving A Good Balance.

The sense that we need to do something even if we don't know why or how to accomplish it is an example of intuitive reasoning. Intuition refers to this kind of unconscious thinking. You have to clear some space in your head and go silent before you can really hear it. A state of quiet, during which the listener focuses inside with the intention of discerning the direction in which they are being led. When you pay attention to your gut instinct and establish a connection with your higher self, you move closer toward being more aligned with the person you were always intended to be.

Everyone have a link to their own intuitive faculties in some form or another. We all know that not everyone pays attention. You are not required to disregard your intelligence; rather, we are working toward striking a healthy balance between your rational thinking and your gut instincts. There is beauty in maintaining a healthy equilibrium. Spend some time on your own, put what you're learning about meditation into practice, and don't forget to remind yourself to actively let go of the negativity and fears that you carry with you. They are an exceedingly heavy load to bear, and the only function they serve is to slow you down and make you feel weighed down.

When we aren't paying attention to it or listening to it, our intuition speaks to us in a soft whisper. Since intuition has nothing to do with your ego, all of the egotistical feelings like wrath, pride, humiliation, and fear are absent from the voice that you hear when you use it. These feelings are loud, strong, and persistent all at the same time. You have the opportunity to make a better decision in the heat of the moment if you push beyond those loud voices and seek out the voice that is calmer, more straightforward, and devoid of any negative emotion. Following your gut instincts is a certain way to become a more genuine version of yourself. Being more genuine makes it impossible for you to ever be in the wrong.

If you want to develop your intuitive abilities and become a more well-rounded person, you should strive to engage in the activities listed below more often:

Put forth some imaginative effort. When you indulge your creative side by doing something like painting, making a piece of jewelry, putting together a scrapbook, writing a song or piece of music, etc., you provide a soothing salve for your spirit. Anything that encourages the development of that aspect of you serves as a source of motivation and strengthens your intuitive abilities.

Continue to develop your ability to be aware. Meditation is the most effective method for accomplishing this goal. The next best thing to do is to quit being so hard on yourself. Accept your experiences for what they are, but try not to be too hard on yourself as a result of them. Pay close attention to it so that you may get a deeper comprehension of it. But refrain from passing judgment.

Learn to recognize and trust your instincts. Pay attention to any and all of the cues that your body sends your way since they are something that should be listened to. Take some time to calm down and focus on figuring out what your body is attempting to tell you at this very moment.

Improve the sense of connection you have with other people. Have you ever been in a situation where the sight of a spider moving over the skin of another person caused your skin to itch? The elation felt by the players and fans of your favorite club after they have been victorious is contagious, isn't it? Try paying attention to someone whose feelings aren't as apparent to you as they normally are. Try reaching out with your own senses to see if you can get a sense of what they are experiencing simply by doing that.

Attend to the voices in your head. If I don't wake up and write down my dreams, I have a hard time remembering what they were like. Because your brain works differently and more instinctively while you're asleep, recording your dreams may provide you with a wealth of useful information that you would not otherwise have access to. In the beginning, they won't make any sense at all. Simply jot them down, and then look for a reliable dream interpretation book or website to consult. Also, keep in mind that the interpretation of dreams is seldom done literally. There are times when divine messages will come to you in your dreams; if you write them down, you will have a much greater chance of understanding what it is that they are trying to convey to you.

Take some time out for yourself, some quiet time to think, work through the things that have transpired, and get rid of any negative ideas that you weren't even aware you had. If you continue to make this decision, you will ultimately discover that you are doing it instinctively, and you will feel lighter, happier, and more joyous as a result.

You have a powerful intuition, and the more consideration you pay to it, the more transparent it will become to you.

Why then did we start the fifth chapter with such a heavy focus on your intuitive abilities? the intuition is connected to the Ajna, often known as the third eye chakra and a topic that has received a lot of attention here. Being receptive to it may lead to clairvoyance, telepathy, lucid dreaming, heightened creativity and imagination, and visualization. It is so many things.

Since before you were born, you have depended on your five senses, which are touch, taste, hearing, sight, and feel. These five senses are what you have relied on. Even when you were still in your mother's womb, you were able to detect her voice and feel her heartbeat. You may depend not just on your five senses but also on your sixth sense, which is intuition. You have, I have no doubt about it. However, this is something that requires practice in order to do continually.

It is difficult for us to place our faith in things that we cannot see, hear, or touch. We are always looking for reinforcement that we are moving in the correct direction with our choices. Where do we direct our gaze? anywhere except from inside ourselves and our own innate patterns of behavior. However, we can make this better. Just like everything else, it requires consistent practice.

One smart strategy would be for us to begin paying a lot more attention to the hints that we are given. When you work out a deal, everything appears terrific and well intentioned, but then comes the time when you shake hands with your counterpart, and all of a sudden the hairs rise up on the back of your hand. This is a sign that something might go wrong with the agreement. Your physical self is trying to alert you to the fact that there is something off about this individual. The transaction is finalized, and you go into business when all of a sudden you realize that it is tainted. Put this in your notebook. When you get a chilling feeling in your body, make a note of it and write down the circumstance at the same time. Then, evaluate both of these things from a fresh point of view. Investigate the matter further and check to see if there is anything you have overlooked. If you are able to make better judgments by paying greater attention to your instincts, then the intuition that you are looking for will get stronger and louder as a result of the fact that you are finally listening to it.

To get through the day, most of us nowadays are dependent on various forms of contemporary technology. It's fairly incredible how much simpler it is for us to do things and organize our lives compared to decades before. Despite this, we are severing ties that we have had in the past, including those with ourselves, our families, nature, and our spirituality. Everything has a cost associated with it.

By and large, people can count on me to be trustworthy. First and foremost, I try to see the best in other people. My sister is extremely wary and skeptical of others, which is the total antithesis of my personality. She, in turn, considers me to be very trusting, and she is concerned that I would place my faith in the incorrect individual. Instead, I worry about her, constantly concentrating on the bad and always preparing myself for the worst possible outcome. She frets so much that something horrible will take place that, when it ultimately occurs, she feels almost elated that she was proved correct all along. She worries so much that something bad will take place.

I try my best to trust my own instincts in the hopes that they will let me know when someone is fundamentally dishonest or does not have my best interests in mind when interacting with me. Is this the case every time? No. I, too, am susceptible to experiencing disappointments, just like everyone else. Despite this, I have made the decision to avoid concentrating on the unfavorable aspects of any one particular individual or circumstance. I am well aware that life is a gift. This life is a blessing that has been bestowed upon us. And if the people you love also love you, then your life is even more full of blessings than it already was. Spend some time appreciating this existence and the people that populate it. Make the most of your time here and take advantage of the intriguing experience that you are now on.

Where did we leave off? Oh sure, striking a balance. I assured you there would be a balance.

Let's put some effort into a workout, shall we?

We are interested in gaining the knowledge necessary to balance our chakras. Meditation is the simplest and most straightforward approach of accomplishing this goal. When you try out these activities, you should pay great attention to everything that you experience. If you feel anything different in your body, it might be a clue that what you're doing is really working.

This is a simple breathing exercise that works wonders for relieving anxiety. It is referred to as brahmari, which is a Sanskrit term that means bee in English. Because of the low buzzing sound that bees produce, this sound has been given its name. Try this out the next time you find yourself feeling apprehensive, and see if it helps. This is another kind of meditation that may be used to open your third eye. One stone may kill two birds.

Put your hands in a cross-like position over your face. Your index fingers should be resting on your eyebrows, and your middle fingers should be placed over each eyelid. It is normal for your pinkies to rest just below your cheekbones. Put your thumbs in your ears and shut your eyes.

Be sure to keep your mouth completely shut. Take a deep breath in through your nose.

As you exhale, sound out the letter "M" in the word "AUM."

Continue to make the sound of the letter M until you feel the desire to take a breath in again.

Take a few deep breaths in through your nose.

Make the sound of a M as you exhale for as long as it is comfortable to do so, releasing your breath while simultaneously creating the sound.

Take a slow, easy breath in.

The M sound should be hummed while exhaling, and you should continue to hum for as long as your lungs will allow without experiencing any pain.

Carry on in this manner for a few more minutes until you get tired.

As soon as you feel ready, go back to your regular breathing pattern. Very gently. Begin to softly open your eyes. Take careful note of how you now feel. It is my hope that some of the anxiety you were experiencing has been alleviated as a result of this. Has the strain left your body? Do you have any tingling sensations?

There are many additional simple techniques you may do to bring balance to your third eye chakra. The child's posture is a simple form of yoga that may help you achieve equilibrium by connecting your third eye to the earth and can also foster the development of your inner eye seeing. The following is a list of yoga positions that are suggested for this task requiring balance.

The Process Of Healing The Seventh Chakra

The seventh chakra, also known as the crown or Sahasrara chakra, may be found at the topmost pinnacle of the head, just above the line of the spine, and at the point where the crown makes contact with the air. It is referred to as the "crowning chakra" not only due to the fact that it is located at the very top of the body, but also due to the fact that it assists in bringing together all of the other chakras, as well as the body, into a single spiritual entity.

The crown chakra, also known as the spiritual chakra, is the point at which the spiritual worlds open up for you, where enlightenment is a possibility, as well as the higher realms of being. It is also known as the point at which the higher realms of being are accessible. By cultivating this chakra, it may be able to achieve spiritual freedom, to communicate with other spiritual beings, and to deepen our mystic experiences. These are all things that might contribute to the development of our spiritual potential. This chakra is the fundamental component of all world faiths and beliefs, and it is the connection point between us and our sense of idealism.

Our brain, namely the cerebrum, cerebellum, and cerebral cortex, as well as our central nervous system, are all related with the crown chakra on a physical level. It controls the pituitary gland and the pineal gland, in addition to all of the hormones that are linked with those organs. When it is in a state of equilibrium, we have gained the ability to overcome our ego, to develop emotional as well as intellectual autonomy, and to be filled with self-assurance since we have accomplished these things.

If the crown chakra is out of alignment, it may cause one to experience emotions of concern, anxiety, issues with confidence, and indifference. This might result in bodily symptoms such as headaches, concern, anxiety, or even diseases of the immune system.

When attempting to cure the seventh chakra, it is imperative that more attention be devoted to the previous chakras as well as the crown chakra itself; focusing just on the crown chakra will not be sufficient. Because it is the last and controlling chakra, it is best to begin from the base of the chakra system and work one's way up towards the crown. Along the way, it is helpful to periodically pause and realign all of the chakras that came before it until we reach the very top. Through this method, we will be able to maintain the crown in its optimal and most fruitful state, serving as a regulator and controller of the whole subtle body.

Exercise for the Throat Chakra:

The following practice will concentrate on the throat chakra, often known as the "anger center," which governs one's capacity to speak out for oneself. Imagine a light blue light moving in a circular manner, either in a clockwise or counterclockwise direction (again, whatever direction seems most natural to you). Keeping visualizing this until it starts moving easily is the goal. When you initially try out these exercises, you shouldn't anticipate that the chakras would feel clear, unobstructed, and straightforward. Depending on how much they have been weakened, it may take more than one attempt for your chakras to start working in a fluid and easy manner again.

Now, visualize the blue light whirling in a clockwise or counterclockwise direction as it travels down your whole body to your feet and then back up again. This process should take place in reverse.

Exercise for the Heart Chakra:

The following exercise will concentrate on the heart chakra, which is located in the middle of your chest and controls not only your capacity to love other people but also your ability to love yourself. Choose either pink or green, since these are the colors associated with the heart chakra; the next activity you do to balance your chakras should use one of these hues.

Imagine that the color you chose—either pink or green—is traveling in either a clockwise or a counterclockwise direction after you have made your selection. When you are ready, begin to move it all the way around your body, all the way down to your feet, and all the way back up to the crown of your head.

Exercise for the Solar Plexus Chakra:

Your solar plexus chakra, which is situated in your diaphragm, is also very closely associated with your emotions. This chakra has a golden hue to its coloration. Again, see a yellow light spinning in a circular motion, this time in either a clockwise or counterclockwise direction, depending on your own choice. Once again, whenever you feel ready, proceed by whirling the yellow light around your body in a clockwise direction, starting at the top of your head and working your way down to your feet.

Exercise for the Sacral Chakra:

The color orange represents the sacral chakra, which is associated with sexuality. Having stated that, visualize an orange light that is traveling in either the clockwise or counterclockwise direction. Once again, when you are ready, swirl the orange light around your body, traveling in an upward direction to the top of your head, and then flowing downward to your feet.

Exercise for the Root Chakra:

In conclusion, the color red represents the root chakra, which is associated with feeling comfortable and secure in all parts of your life. This chakra is located at the base of the spine. Your pelvic region is the location of the root chakra, which stands for the roots of your family and where you came from. For the sake of this exercise, visualize a crimson light whirling about in the region of your body that contains this chakra; in this example, the area of your pelvis. After that, move this light in a spiral motion all the way down and back up your body.

A human being has to have a balance between the upward flow of energy and the downward flow of energy in order to be entire, which includes feeling like they are in excellent form both mentally and physically. The purpose of these exercises is to increase the flow of energy through the chakras, making it possible for it to flow more freely and with greater ease, which ultimately results in the chakras being more balanced and better.

By meditating with Color Therapy and frequently doing these exercises, the healing color and light of the universe will be brought into your spiritual being. As a result, you will feel happier, healthier, more serene, and more able to easily take control over the problems that are now occurring in your life.

4. THE HEART CHAKRA, OTHERWISE KNOWN AS THE ANAHATA

It is at the level of the heart, as the name of the structure indicates. It connects the three chakras below it with the three chakras above it, serving as a bridge between the seven chakras. It is fundamental to achieving one's own goals and serves as the springboard for the emotions of love and compassion. In the same way that an abundance of energy may generate an abundance of these sensations, a lack of energy can cause feelings of envy, anger, and paranoia. Some of the physical problems that are connected to the heart chakra include conditions such as heart disease and back discomfort.

It is advised that one practices meditation with the intention of rebalancing the energy by concentrating on the center of the heart while envisioning a golden sphere that encircles the whole body. Rosewood, cypress, lavender, patchouli, and ylang-ylang are some of the essential oils that are suggested for use throughout the session.

5. THE THROAT CHAKRA, ALSO CALLED THE VISHUDDHA CHAKRA

The entrance of the gorge is home to what is known as the throat chakra, which is associated with expression and creativity. It enables the expression of ideas, information, and emotions to the outside world, both verbally and via gestures. An excess of energy may cause haughtiness, a failure to listen, and mythomania, while a blockage can make it difficult to express oneself and make one feel uncertain about their abilities. Pain in the neck, headaches, and problems with the thyroid gland are all symptoms that may be caused by an imbalance.

When you meditate, bring your attention to the path that runs from the bottom of the heart to the top of the head, passing through the neck on its way. It is essential to take slow, deep breaths and picture a blue light moving in a circular motion through all three of these zones. From inside the body. The following essential oils should be utilized: lemon, cypress, incense, geranium, peppermint (either green or peppery), and sage.

6. THE THIRD EYE CHAKRA, OTHERWISE KNOWN AS THE AJNA

The third eye chakra, which is located in the space between the brows, is associated with self-awareness, sensory perception, and creativity. It is sometimes referred to as the sixth sense and enables individuals to develop their healing ability over themselves as well as others (at a distance). A shortage of energy may cause blindness, dyslexia, and learning issues, as well as a lack of intuition, personality, and extrasensory talents. An excess of energy can lead to narcissism and the intellectual superiority complex.

During meditation, one should concentrate on reestablishing a connection with one's body while also paying attention to the indicators that exist outside of the body. It is essential to put your faith in your instincts and pay attention to the advice your soul gives you. Lemon, sandalwood, incense, juniper, bay leaf, patchouli, rosemary, and clary sage are the essential oils that should be used.

7. THE CHAKRA OF THE CROWN, ALSO CALLED SAHASRARA

It is the energy of enlightenment that links every human being to the cosmos, and it is located at the very top of the head, at the top of the skull. It opens the door to our subconcious and unconscious selves, allowing us to become mindful of the beauty in all that surrounds us. If having too much energy gives you headaches and makes you feel frustrated, you may have too little of it, which may lead to a lack of awareness of spirituality. Both suicidal thoughts and the inability to remember past events may be traced back to an imbalance in the Sahasrara chakra.

Through the practice of meditation, one may establish a connection with their mind. During the process, it is essential to picture a light engulfing the crown of the head. This light is meant to energize both the physical and spiritual bodies. Lime, cedar wood, sandalwood, helichrysum, gurjum, lavender, and rose are some of the other essential oils that should be prioritized.

Meditations Using Chakra Mantras To Release Blocked Energy

Sound is a kind of vibration. Mantras that are known to be in vibrational harmony with each chakra may be used for the goals of opening up the system and bringing it back into balance. This is something that you may not be aware of, since each of your chakras also has its own unique frequency.

During meditation, reciting certain mantras associated with each chakra may have a very significant impact. Imagine a chakra to be a utensil and a mantra to be a tuning fork; when you hit the tuning fork, the utensil will come into vibrational resonance with it, unblocking any energies that do not share the same resonance as the tuning fork.

There are five seed mantras.

Let's start with some of the most fundamental mantras, which are known as bija mantras, sometimes known as seed mantras, and which have been utilized over the ages in meditation practices to bring one's energy into balance.

OM: (which is pronounced "Aum") The most well recognized and ubiquitous of all the bija mantras. It is the sound of creation, also known as the anahatnaad, and it causes energy to accumulate and flow upward into the crown chakra and forth into the cosmos. Acceptance and submission are represented by the mantra OM. It assists us in accepting our greater selves and opening up channels for energy to flow openly and freely throughout. It also functions as a collecting mantra, allowing you to gather your inside energy and get it ready for action.

KRIM (pronunciation: "kreem"): When we chant this mantra, we encourage our lower chakras to awaken, which then begins the process of cleaning our body by elevating its vibrations.

(Pronounced "shreem") SHRIM: It is associated with the head, specifically the third eye. It not only helps one become physically and spiritually aware, but it can also be utilized to beautify one's being and offer joy to one's senses.

The word "HRIM" (pronounced "hreem") refers to anything that has the ability to heal and inspire creativity. This mantra brings about an awakening of compassion and cleanses the heart as it is spoken.

HUM (pronounced "hoom"): This elicits the dissolution of negative sentiments and distributes optimism and vigor throughout the body.

After reading the list, choose the mantra(s) to which you feel an instinctive pull and pick one or more of them. Your body has seven chakras, and each of the cleaning mantras correlates to one of those chakras. You may be highly "energetically healthy" in certain ways and not so much in others, so there is no need to worry about employing all of them.

Simply choose the one that speaks to your requirements (you can ask yourself, "Does this sound helpful to me?"), and then use it as a springboard to start your meditation practice. This figuratively "settles the score" for your meditation, after which you may absorb the curative energies of the purifying mantras that have been presented in this article.

Concerning The Area Of The Sacral Chakra

The sacral chakra, also known as Svadhistana, may be found on a person's body just below the naval region. The term "Svadhistana" originates from the Sanskrit words "swa," which means "one's own," and "adhistana," which means "dwelling place within." Together, these words form the English word "Svadhistana." Deep feelings, like as desire, pleasure, and sexuality, are connected to the chakra known as Svadhistana. It is the hub of all reproductive activity. Its location around the naval area, which is a particularly sensitive portion of the human body, is evidence of its nature as a sensory chakra. This region of the body is found around the navel. As a result of the fact that this part of the body is also the part of the body in which water is most abundant, the element that corresponds to this chakra is water.

This chakra is also known as the lover's chakra since it is mostly related with sex and the aforementioned sensations that result from sex, such as passion and pleasure. It is also known as the heart chakra because it is located at the center of the chest. Its connotations are considerably lighter than those of the Muladhara, which was covered in the chapter before this one, and it focuses more on the exploration of emotional depths like as curiosity and invigoration than on the exploration of fundamental instinctive demands. Orange is the hue that corresponds to this sensation, and the sense of taste is the one that is connected with it. The uterus, testicles, pelvis, and lower back are all under the jurisdiction of the sacral chakra.

Each of the six petals that make up the Svadhistana visualization is in charge of a distinct unpleasant feeling. This does not mean that meditating on the sacral chakra can remove these petals, but it may help restore balance to the energies that are contained inside the chakra. As a result of the fact that positive cannot exist without negative, the emotions are already present. Therefore, it is our duty as spiritual beings to take charge of our emotions, whether they be happy or bad, rather than allowing them to direct our behavior.

The Primordial Sounds Resonating Within the Sacral Chakra

The first sound of the Svadhistana is a 'vum.' One particular feeling or disposition is represented by each individual petal. The uppermost petal is referred to as 'prashraya,' and it is responsible for determining your level of credulity. The following petal is called 'avishvasa,' and it is located below the previous one in the clockwise direction. This petal regulates the predisposition you have to distrust other people. The next petal is called 'avajna,' and it is in charge of the feeling that causes one person to feel contempt for another person. Bewilderment is represented by the middle of the bottom petal, which is called "murchha." The next petal is called sarvanasha, and it marks the beginning of an ascent while proceeding around the flower in a clockwise orientation. This petal is the one a one should blame for their destructive tendencies. The ultimate petal is known as 'krurata,' and it is the one that is accountable for cruelty. If you want to meditate on a certain chakra, you should vocalize the corresponding root sound that corresponds to each of the chakra's seven petals. The first consonant of the word 'prashraya' is 'bham,' 'avishvasa' is the same as 'bham,' The word 'avajna' may be pronounced as 'mam,' 'murchha' can be spoken as 'yam,' 'sarvanasha' can be pronounced as 'ram,' and 'krurata' can be pronounced as 'lam.'

It is stated that a person who meditates on these sounds has a great sense of self-esteem since they have vanquished all of their internal adversaries and won prosperity and light. When you focus your meditation on the sacral chakra, you let go of issues that have something to do with acceptance of the self, anti-social conduct, and co-dependency, which ultimately leads to a greater sense of self-awareness.

These Are the Seven Primary Chakras

Chakra de l'origine

Your Root chakra may be located in the base of your spine, which most people can feel in the small of their back. The color of this chakra, which is also known as the Base chakra, is a deep ruby red, very similar to the hue of a red laser light.

This chakra, which is referred to as Muladhara in Sanskrit, is responsible for keeping you rooted in the material sensations of life, survival, and instincts. It also influences fundamental feelings such as ambition, rage, and desire.

The region of the sacral chakra

Even though it is located quite near to the navel, this chakra is not often activated while one is navel gazing. You may locate it by holding two fingers below your belly button in a horizontal position. It lies tucked away at the tip of your lower finger, where it glows a vivid orange and spins like the dark core of a blazing fire or the sun at dawn and dusk.

This chakra, which influences both sexuality and creativity, is known in Sanskrit as Svadhishthana. It is essential for creative people, such as artists and other persons who express themselves sexually. Even while all of your chakras are necessary to bring your manifestations into the physical world, the sacral chakra is the primary engine that propels the majority of what you bring into existence.

Chakra of the Solar Plexus

Your solar plexus is located just below your ribcage, in the little depression that is just above your stomach. This is the natural location of your solar plexus chakra. The hue of this center is a bright and cheery yellow. In the manner of a sunflower or a gorgeous, transparent citrine gemstone.

This chakra, which is referred to as Manipura in Sanskrit, has an effect on your feeling of power as well as your self-esteem and sense of identity. Accessing your daily intuition or 'gut' feeling, as well as 'digesting' emotions and experiences, are all essential components of healthy material manifestation. The heart chakra plays an important role in all of these areas.

Your Heart chakra, which can be easily felt, is located in line with the other chakras and your actual heart. This is the region that theatrical individuals like to grasp in order to indicate how intensely they are experiencing something. The color of your Heart chakra is a rich emerald green, quite similar to the color of the "go" sign on traffic lights.

Your ability to feel and express love and compassion is impacted by your Heart chakra, which is referred to in Sanskrit as Anahata. In addition to this, it is the engine that propels your capacity to heal and connect with the planet and the creatures who surround you.

Chakra de la Throat

This chakra is located in the centre of your neck, roughly in the area where a man's Adam's apple would be. It is another chakra that is simple to locate. Its hue resembles a crystal-clear indigo. Imagine shades of blue like sapphire and clear sky.

This blue chakra, which is associated with your capacity to communicate and tell your truth, is referred to in Sanskrit as the Vishuddha chakra.

The Chakra of the Third Eye

This well-known and shrouded energy center may be found in the exact center of your forehead. It has a hue that may be described as indigo or a rich, pure purple.

In Sanskrit, this faculty is referred to as Ajna, and it plays a critical role in how you see the world and the people in it. This chakra is the source of your more advanced intuition.

The sacral energy center

The next chakra center that we will investigate is the one that is associated with our interests and gratifications. The Svadhistana Chakra, also known as the Sacral Chakra, is in charge of how you personally experience life. In the end, everything boils down to your physical sensations and the emotions you feel, and how those two things link you to other people. The fact that the chakra center itself is situated in the pelvic region should not come as much of a surprise given the connection that the Sacral chakra has with sexual energy. Because of this, the reproductive systems and the act of procreation in general are considered to be components of the Svadhistana. The color orange is said to be associated with this chakra point.

Your sacral chakra acts as a personal key that may be used to open doors that lead to your unique creative potential. We have already discussed how the Sacral chakra is the origin of passion, and because passion is the driving force behind creativity, it seems sense that both passion and creativity originate from the same chakra center. Although each person's creative abilities are unique due to their beliefs, upbringing, and the society in which they are immersed, it is possible for anybody to improve their creative abilities via the practice of meditation and exercise focused on the chakra centers themselves. This chakra is most developed in children because of their capacity to play for extended periods of time without tiring, as well as their lack of self-restraint in terms of how they feel and how they express themselves. Adults that resonate strongly with this chakra center are often creative types, such as painters or musicians, or they have libidos that are much higher than average. It is quite simple to overindulge in the Svadhistana, which may lead to the chakra itself being imbalanced. This is because of the nature of the chakra itself.

An imbalanced amount of sacral energy may lead to the development of unhealthy preoccupations or addictions with items that provide a heightened sense of pleasure. Sexual dysfunction and promiscuity are also quite frequent adverse effects associated with this medication. These detrimental new behaviors are likely to leave the individual feeling an overwhelming sense of guilt, which may often lead to melancholy in the affected person. Problems with the kidneys, the prostate, or the urinary and gynecological regions are some examples of other physical characteristics that may become apparent. Additionally, emotional sensitivity becomes a problem, which results in a rise in the number of outbursts and fits of wrath. If one were to let things go unchecked for long enough, it's probable that they would harden their heart and lose their sensitivity, but it's not hard to stop such things from happening.

Utilizing positive affirmations that zero in on the components that are most important to balancing your Sacral chakra is the simplest approach to get started on the process. You are the only one who can make things work for you by having the belief and determination to make it happen, therefore you may either make them yourself or look for ones that already exist. The second method for stimulating this chakra center is to simply surround oneself with the color orange. This will assist. Take a bath in water that has been colored orange with food coloring for a therapy that is not only soothing but also beneficial. This works in part because of the color, and in part because water is the element that is linked with the Svadhistana chakra. In addition to being beneficial for one's general health, working out the abdominal muscles is an excellent approach to stimulate the Sacral chakra. Consuming meals with an orange coloration can help stimulate this chakra center, which is a sensory kind, and will also assist in getting your chakra into high gear. When you combine this with a few yoga positions each day, not only will you notice an increase in the flow of your energy, but you will also develop a healthier lifestyle, which will allow you to live longer and take more pleasure in the activities you most like.

The second way is to breathe.

Never underestimate the power of a good, lengthy inhale and exhale, especially if you are trying to release something from your body. The appropriate breathing methods and practices may help you release a lot from your body. It's true that breathing may cure you; in fact, it's far more potent than you would imagine.

After coming across the account of Miki Ryosuke, a Japanese actor who had back discomfort and was recommended to do some breathing methods to release the relief, he did start performing some breathing practices and was astounded by the fact that he lost weight through breathing alone. Now, his tale is quite well known, and he has developed a diet called the Miki Ryosuke's diet, which provides instructions on how to reduce body fat using breathing techniques.

I believe that every person is going to get something different from breathing practices. For example, if two people started practicing breathing, one might experience a collagen boost and wrinkles fading from his face while the other might get a childhood trauma out of his system. Breathing is not going to give everyone the same result, and I believe that every person is going to get something different from breathing practices.

Use it, think about it, and thank the god of the universe for this gift that is freely provided and that you may exercise whenever you want since it is an excellent method of letting go that doesn't cost anything. Also, don't expect for results to manifest from the very first day; give it some time since blockages don't develop overnight; it takes months, if not years, to feel and obtain the consequence of a blocked energy point, so let healing and releasing entirely to take time; dedication is really important in this process.

The concept that breath is a life-giver and that life is contained within breath itself is central to Sufism, which places a strong emphasis on the significance of breath. It is an essential instrument for healing, and when a person exudes rage and flame, the breath becomes the fire that they emit. Sufism teaches that breath is God and that God is expressed in breath, and it even indicates that the quality of one's breath is directly related to one's level of physical and mental health. A person may go for days without drinking water or eating food, but they can only go for seconds without breathing, which highlights the significance of this bodily function. The power of breath is used by the Sufi in order to connect with the supreme deity and to maintain presence in the present moment.

It is said that through breathing in this type of practice many things are manifested such as: - Slowing down the aging process, boosting the body's collagen - Creativity gets activated and IQ level is increased - Feeling cleansed and purified, free of traumas and negative energies - Being more aware and having better senses - Slowing down the aging process, boosting the body's collagen - Slowing down the aging process, boosting the body's collagen

- A calm condition of both the mind and the body

This kind of yoga places a significant emphasis on the breath. Through proper breathing, miraculous healing may take place, and cellular renewal can take place.

"The breath travels around the body in a circle, and the spine serves as the path that the breath travels along to complete the circle. The mystics place a tremendous deal of significance on this channel, which they refer to as the snake. The image they see in their heads is of a snake with its tail in its jaws. Almost wherever you look, you'll see a snake depicted as the conduit for the air we breathe. Kundalini is the phrase that Yogis use to refer to this energy. When this channel is made clear by the technique of breathing, then this is not only helpful to the physical health, but it also opens up the faculties of intuition and the doors that are inside, which is where the true happiness of man resides. When this channel is made clear, then the method of breathing. One must adhere to the norms of mystical ablutions and rhythmic breathing in order to rid this channel of anything that stands in the way of progress. - Chapter 13, Gathas Vol.

The Heart Chakra

The color green is used to signify the heart chakra, and just as the hue says, this chakra is all about maintaining good relationships as well as love, affection, and caring for others. If you are able to open this specific chakra, you will find that you are more inclined to lead a joyful life. An open heart chakra will allow you to get the most out of your relationships and ensure that the people who are linked to you are content. It will also allow you to feel compassion for the people around you. To put it another way, the power of this chakra is such that it has an impact not only on you but also on the individuals in your immediate environment. You will be well loved, and the Chakra has the potential to even elevate your status among your peers.

On the other side, having a closed heart or a heart chakra that is just partially open may lead to feelings of emptiness, particularly when discussing personal connections and those with whom one is familiar. You will become hostile and resistant to attending social events if your heart chakra is closed. Because you are closed off to other people, they will respond to you with the same lack of emotion that they have towards you. After all, everything you give out will eventually come back to you.

A person who has an overactive heart chakra will have an excessive capacity for love and compassion. Because of this specific quality, the individuals around you are likely to experience feelings of suffocation and a great deal of discomfort. When you start challenging the beliefs of those closest to you and demanding answers from them, they are going to start ignoring you as a result. Despite the fact that you seem to be a lovely person, this will give the impression that you are intrusive and inquisitive. You may think that having a heart chakra that is overactive is unhealthy for long-term partnerships.

The following description is of a simple practice that may assist in opening one's heart chakra. It is important to keep in mind that for our bodies to be able to express and experience love and relationships in a way that is most conducive to human behaviors, the heart chakra must be open and functioning properly. Keeping this information in mind, you should cross your legs and sit on a surface that is level, ideally on the ground.

Put your hands on your knees, bring the points of both of your thumbs together so that they meet the tips of your index fingers, and then spread the rest of your fingers out in a straight line. After you have given yourself some time to relax, bring your right hand to your chest and keep it there in the same position, making sure that it is in the middle of your chest and near to your heart. You should not move your fingers and thumbs into a different position.

It is time for you to relax, and you will get there by clearing everything out of your thoughts. Consider the advantages associated with the heart chakra and keep it in mind. You should make an effort to envision your heart and spine in a relaxed state without causing yourself or the procedure any stress. Start reciting the "YAM" mantra as soon as you feel that you have regained your balance and calm.

If you allow your thoughts to wander and get preoccupied with things of this world, the power of this chant will not be able to work as intended. It is essential that you keep repeating the heart mantra to yourself and that you place a strong emphasis on the idea that whatever you are doing is gently and gradually making your heart cleaner. Just try to picture how calm and content you will be after you have properly opened your heart chakra.

Carry on with this exercise until you begin to feel good about yourself and until you acquire that "clean" sensation on the interior of your body.

Another item that is worth emphasizing here is something that is pretty obvious: this exercise need to be done in a quiet setting in which the possibilities of being distracted are minimized. The best time to do this is either first thing in the morning or just before you go to bed. In most cases, at this time of day, the environment around you is quiet and tranquil.

Disharmonies in the Crown Chakra

When our Crown chakra is blocked, we may experience feelings of spiritual disconnection as well as cynicism. It's possible for us to feel dread of death and a sense that we aren't worthy of plenty, along with apprehension about the future and a lack of purpose. If our Crown chakra is hyperactive, we may have a tendency to be too philosophical or to have a "head in the clouds" manner of thinking. It's possible that we would rather often be in a state of meditation than be firmly rooted in the here and now. The inability to remember things in the short term, a lack of muscular coordination, and problems with the neurological system are some of the physical symptoms that may result from an imbalance in the seventh chakra.

Minerals, Rocks, and Crystals

We may use crystals that are either clear, white, or purple in color to bring about harmony in the Crown chakra by working with these colors. Just a few examples of possible stones are amethyst, selenite, and clear or rutilated quartz. During meditation, you may either choose to hold these stones in your hands or position them straight over your head.

Foods and Spices

Foods that are high in alkalinity, such as leafy greens, avocados, celery, and beets, are excellent sources of sustenance for the Crown chakra in our bodies. Consuming only natural, organic foods may also assist in maintaining the openness and equilibrium of the Crown chakra. Holy basil, St. John's wort, and pink lotus are some of the herbs that are known to be beneficial to this chakra.

The Practices Of Yoga And Traditional Chinese Medicine

By participating in various hands-on activities at this stage of the process, we will be able to get a more in-depth understanding of the meridians that run through our bodies. This will allow us to develop a more personal connection to these energy pathways. In each and every class, we will go further into an aspect that will enable us to work on two meridians at the same time while they are paired. In addition to the yoga movements that we will be working on, we will also be working on meridian stretching activities.

In order to further aid the comprehension of the Chinese vision of the organs that belong to the lodges, as well as to get a grasp of the significance and function of each element, a quick explanation of the key features will be provided in the following short paragraphs.

There will be a listing of some of the Chinese's most important correspondences for each element. This listing will take into consideration the analogical reasoning that the Chinese used while classifying things.

3) Make a bed of soil. The SPLIT/PANCREAS and the STOMACH meridians are coupled. Interstellar periods and the energy of the cosmos YELLOW is the color. CONNECTIVE TEXTILES Fabrics roles of the senses: the MOUTH Sweet is the flavor. odors of a PERFUMED nature BAVA Are the Secretions. utterances: a SONG REFLECTION on the physical and physiological conditions that are present

Pathological mental states characterized by CONCERN

4) Install the METAL. The LUNGS and the LARGE INTESTINE are coupled meridians. energy from the cosmos: AUTUMN WHITES is the color. Skin (as a tissue) Functions of the senses: NOSE Flavors: HOT AND SPICY Nauseabondo is the odor. MUCO NASALE and PLANT are the sounds that are produced. states both physiological and psychological: UNSTRUCTURED Mental disorders that are pathological: SADNESS

The WATER Lodge, number 5. Kidneys and the bladder are examples of coupled meridians. The energy of the cosmos: WINTER BLACK is the color. Materials: BONE Functions of the senses: hearing and the ears SALTED is the flavor. SMELLS OF MOLD SALIVA: A MISSION TO YOU The sound of a lament Biological and psychological states: WILLING

Disorders of the mind that are pathological: FEAR

5 Hydrotherapic Treatment

In every civilization that has ever been, water has been one of the natural elements, after the earth and the sun, that has most attracted the curiosity of the people. Its application has often covered both magical and medicinal properties, and its usage has been known to have both of these effects.

It's likely that people have been using water to treat illnesses and maintain their health ever before civilization was created. Hippocrates, a Greek physician who lived in the fifth century B.C., advocated drinking the water from the spring due to the positive benefits it had on one's health. According to a practice that the ancient Romans endeavored to propagate across the whole of the Empire, they went to the public baths with such fervor that they constructed magnificent structures that were both roomy and beautiful in order to accommodate their intricate aquatic rituals.

It has long been thought that the water from certain springs has therapeutic benefits and may heal various ailments; the spas that emerged in the seventeenth century mostly attract individuals who are searching for a routine that allows them to rest and rejuvenate themselves.

In addition to its usage for thermal purposes, water is put to use in a wide variety of therapeutic and aesthetic activities. These vary from cold baths to barefoot walks on wet grass, from fasts based on thermal water to the hydro-massages that are now all the rage. Water-based treatments are an integral part of the field of naturopathy.

The arsenal of hydrotherapy treatments was increased in the eighteenth and nineteenth centuries with the procedures that are still believed to be more productive now. This took place throughout those eras. In the first place, it was the work of V. Priessnitz, the Austrian healer who became known as "the genius of cold water," and of the Bavarian abbot S. Kneipp, who was the primary popularizer of Priessnitz methods.

Kneipp was so confident in the body's capacity to heal itself that he built a clinic that specialized in hydrotherapy, which included treatments such as hot and cold baths, steam baths, compresses, showers, and foot baths. In addition, patients were required to adhere to a rigorous diet and engage in rigorous physical activity. Water and earth, in addition to the effect of materials from the atmosphere and the cosmos, are the key components of the whole of the living organism's biological and morphological structure.

In reality, the human body is composed of 74% water, which is also true for plant species. Water is the primary component of every biological animal and plant form, and this holds true for both plant and animal life. Water is a crucial component for the existence of the body. This is true not only because it satisfies our thirst and allows us to clean ourselves with it, but also because it is the component that drives biological metabolism and acts as its vehicle.

In point of fact, during the process of nutrition, it takes part in all of the metabolic functions, both in the biochemical phenomena of dissolution of nutritional substances and in the transport of those substances; it also takes part in the saline and humoral balance, acting as a vehicle in the excretory means or the elimination of the substances of organic residue or waste; and finally, it plays a role in the transport of these substances.

Water is an essential component of the biochemical and physiological processes that occur inside the body. In addition to the reasons that have previously been discussed, this is due to the fact that water governs the body's complete nutritional, biochemical, and physiological system via the process of osmosis, which promotes chemical and electrical exchanges. Both people and animals have, from the beginning of time, intuitively realized the inherent healing characteristics that water has, and have used it as a medicinal ingredient for the purpose of health recovery and maintenance.

The use of water and mud poultices in accordance with three key principles that each govern the same number of physiological processes distinguishes hydrothermofangotherapy from other forms of poultice-based therapies:

The first principle addresses the anti-inflammatory process, also known as the decongestion of the inflammation. This decongestion may be partial or directed depending on the requirements of the situation. The second tenet is based on the neurological response of vasoconstriction and vasodilation, also known as the process that controls the circulation of blood throughout the whole body, including the intestines and the skin, and which goes by the term thermoregulation.

The third principle entails the process or phenomena of osmosis, which is the function that governs the humoral exchange of the organic substances contained in the vascular system of the blood and lymph, as well as that of the digestive, renal, and interstitial regions of the flesh muscular tissue. Osmosis is the function that regulates the humoral exchange of the organic substances contained in the vascular system of the blood and lymph.

In addition, when administered using the techniques of hydrofangiotherapy, water and mud have an effect that is both tonic and regenerative on the nervous system. The practice of using water to which natural ingredients have been added for medicinal reasons is referred to as hydrotherapy.

It is possible to use it at a wide range of temperatures, including cold (not icy), warm, hot, or even extremely hot, or to the limit of one's endurance (in this case, only for exterior use). In addition to being used in either a cold or warm state, the water may also be supplemented with decoctions and infusions of therapeutic herbs, as well as repulsive or naturally fragrant compounds, according on the therapeutic goals and the physiological state of the body.

The Base Chakra

Our link to the ground is maintained by the Base Chakra, which sits at the very bottom of the spine. It has an effect on our libido as well as the lower portions of our body, including the pelvis, rectum, legs, feet, and gonads. It also provides support for our skeletal, neurological, and immunological systems. The earth is the element associated with the Base Chakra, and it is the chakra that is responsible for our connection to the physical world. Using our five senses to help us orient ourselves in space and time, its energy is centered on ensuring our continued existence, safety, and security. In order to maintain a healthy Base Chakra, you need to ground yourself in logic, order, and structure.

The Base Chakra, which is also referred to as the tribal chakra, is the energy center that is in charge of assisting us in defining who we are by pointing us in the direction of our appropriate position within the context of our family and community. It's possible that biological relatives, acquaintances, religious connections, our socioeconomic status, our national identity, and our ethnic origins might all be considered members of the same family or tribe. All of these relationships have an impact on the beliefs and values that guide our lives. The chisels that are used to carve out our characters are the members of our families. They not only give emotional and psychological stability, but also instruct us in the ethical standards by which we should live. The stability of our Base Chakra is dependent on whether or not our family or tribe is able to provide us with the necessities of life, such as food, water, shelter, and a feeling that we belong. The effect of this equilibrium is a sense of having power over oneself. We have a strong sense of being centered and anchored in our bodies.

It is possible for there to be either a deficiency or a surplus of energy associated with the Base Chakra in a familial or tribal setting that is dysfunctional. When our Base Chakra is blocked, we experience a devastating lack of self-confidence, helplessness in the face of the obstacles of physical reality, and the false notion that we are unwanted. An unhealthy obsession on the material elements of life is brought on by excessive stimulation of the Base Chakra. This leads to the development of a dominant, egotistical personality as well as a greedy addiction to amassing riches. The inability to maintain a healthy balance in the Base Chakra may result in a variety of medical ailments, including constipation, kidney stones, and urinary tract infections.

Our families are typically the source of the restricting ideals and harmful habits that are the root cause of the negative patterns that we experience in our lives. When we were younger, we relied on our family for support, but now that we are adults working for our own personal objectives, we need to reconsider the lessons that our families imparted to us. We have a responsibility to recognize our good inheritances and make good use of them. At the same time, we have a responsibility to recognize our bad inheritances and eliminate them from our life.

When we are trying to bring our Base Chakras back into balance, we need to work through any interpersonal problems we have with members of our family or tribe. Take a good, hard look at the societal mores, morals, and traditions that you picked up from your parents and grandparents. Consider whether or not they are still relevant now. Consider the characteristics that were passed down to you and ask yourself which ones help you succeed and which ones hold you back. Consider how you might put an end to the power battles that occur inside your family ties. The reorganization of family dynamics and the assumption of personal responsibility for one's own well-being, safety, and continued existence are two of the most important steps in the process of balancing the Base Chakra. When you balance the Base Chakra, you stabilize the basis upon which all other elements of your life are built.

Raise the Stakes!

It is essential that you take care of your body and engage in activities that will maintain your muscles healthy and powerful. Maintaining your muscle tone is an effective method for doing this, and doing so will also make it easier for you to break free of any clutching tendencies that are caused by your muscles.

Yoga not only gets your body ready for meditation but also turns it into a vessel for your soul to go through. It is an excellent instrument that may assist you in toning. A common problem area that has to be toned is the region of the lower abdominals. There are a number of great yoga postures that may help you tone the abdominal muscles, including the boat pose and the pendant pose.

Act as though no one is seeing you and dance.

The Sacral Chakra and the Root Chakra may be opened up in one of the simplest and most effective ways by dancing. Turn on some music, close the door, and concentrate simply on moving your body. You may achieve harmony in your Root Chakra with this method, which is both effective and simple.

Don't be shy about joining in the singing. Singing is an excellent way to clear up your Throat Chakra. It doesn't matter whether there is music playing; what matters is that you start moving your body.

Bring each of your Chakras back into alignment.

Because your chakras function as a system, an imbalance in one will often produce an imbalance in another; thus, it is important to strive toward achieving balance in each of your chakras.

The first, or Base, or Root Chakra

This Chakra is located at the bottom of the spine, at the tailbone. If you apply some common sense to the situation, you may deduce that this factor contributes to both the survival of the organism and its feeling of equilibrium. This is the chakra that provides the subject with a feeling of independence, and it is also possible to classify it as a chakra that determines a person's financial status, stature, and social position.

From the concise explanations presented above, you may deduce that each Chakra serves a certain function. It's not nearly as difficult as finding the right acupressure point in your body. In point of fact, it is a lot less complicated in comparison to the acupuncture pressure points that are used to map out the whole body. If one of the chakras does not let energy to flow properly through the body, then the individual will suffer in some manner. The chakras are the centers of wellness, and if one of them does not allow energy to flow correctly through the body, then the other chakras will not too.

Because of this, it is clear that the ideal situation is to have chakras that are balanced and a lifestyle that supports each of the chakras so that a human being can benefit the most from the energy flow through their body. This energy flow includes the energy that is used to seek out spiritual understanding as well as the energy that is used to carry out the primary functions of the body and the emotions that it may go through.

If you want to make the most of your energy and also understand how these chakras were developed and what the historical backdrop is behind the knowledge of how they operate, it may be useful to research more extensively. The chakra system was discovered many years before the Buddha, despite the fact that Buddhism is largely based on what the Buddha learned.

Bringing Back The Sense Of Balance To The Heart Chakra

When it comes to regaining a healthy balance in your heart chakra, the natural world is one of your most reliable partners. Spend as much time as possible walking in the woods or on the beach, spending as much time outside as you can when you can.

Also, prioritize quality time with the people you care about the most. This may assist the Heart Chakra in "remembering" its role and functioning more appropriately going forward. Spend the day catching up with your loved ones, but don't forget about your pals too. Spending time with the individuals who are important to you will help you maintain your equilibrium.

Green beverages and meals, as well as green essential oils, may all contribute to the recharging of the Heart Chakra.

This is the Throat Chakra.

It should come as no surprise that the throat houses this chakra since it is associated with speech and expression.

What exactly is the function of the Throat Chakra?

This chakra is responsible for regulating both your speech and your beliefs. Because of this energy, you are able to express your thoughts and worries, even if they run counter to what other people think and say.

Both your inner and your outside voices are given more force when you work with the Throat chakra.

Warning Signs That Your Throat Chakra Is Out of Balance

If the energy in your Throat Chakra is unbalanced, you may find it challenging to communicate with others in a straightforward manner. When it comes time for you to articulate your ideas and viewpoints in front of other people, nervousness will get in the way and make it difficult for you to do so.

It's also possible that you'll start mistrusting other people, which, in turn, will make you less loyal to the individuals who are essential to you. This cycle will continue until you reach rock bottom.

Where do the chakras come from?

Human beings, or Homo sapiens, are the most incredible organisms that have ever existed. A human being's energy field is the conduit via which their life force flows. The energy force is located in this core, which is known as the chakra. The term "turning" or "wheel" in its literal sense is whence we get the word "chakra," which was borrowed from a Sanskrit word. Because they are located inside the body, some refer to them as the "wheels of life." These vortices of energy are known as chakras, and they are located at certain points throughout the human body. They are the channels via which the energy enters and exits your body, and they are represented by your auras. You are aware that detritus, leaves, litter, dirt, and waste constantly obstruct the streams and lakes, right? It is the same with the chakras since they are capable of being blocked by a variety of various sorts of energy. Because of this, it is really necessary for you to continue working on the chakras and to strive toward maintaining them clean. You will not be able to attain the utmost degree of fitness in terms of your physical appearance, spirituality, or mind until you do this, since it is the only way to do so.

The author Rosalyn Bruyere explains the connection between the auras and the chakras in her book Wheels of Light: Chakras, Auras, and the Healing Energy of the Body. Bruyere also discusses the healing energy of the body. She had said that a person should consider his or her trip to be something conventional rather than innovative. These chakras, which are filled with an incredible amount of electromagnetic energy, have been around for as long as Mother Earth has! These chakras were once a key component of long-forgotten mysteries, but those secrets have been lost to time. The second thing that you will need to keep in mind is that you will find your way back to a secret that is at least as old as the existence of life on this planet by means of these chakras. God is the name of this mystery.

As soon as you begin to focus on developing your chakras, you will realize that you are thrust into an extraordinary adventure. You will be able to focus the energy of light that is already inside you, and you will also be able to let go of any responsibilities or burdens that you may be carrying through life. When you maintain the equilibrium of your chakras, you will not only be able to keep yourself healthy but also joyful. You are going to need to work on your meditation, and you are also going to need to practice the methods that are presented in this book. You will also be able to restore balance to the energy centers that are located throughout your body. You will discover that you are capable of healing yourself on all levels, including the physical, the mental, and the spiritual. You will also have a greater capacity to comprehend oneself, and in the course of doing so, you will locate and awaken your spiritual self.

You will notice that each chakra is always connected with a hue that is unique to it. This is something that you should keep in mind. These consistently correlate to the colors of the rainbow, with red appearing at the bottom and violet appearing at the very top. Because you are about to go through an energy vortex, you could notice that your experiences have several tiers to them.

When you are working on your chakras, you will discover that there are seven different styles of meditation that you might practice. These stretches aren't only for the chakras; everybody may benefit from them. Your body has a number of energy centers known as chakras, and you may repair and restore balance to these areas via a variety of activities. It is common practice to correlate these chakras with a person's physical, emotional, and mental well-being. However, there are several perspectives about the ways in which the chakras might be associated with certain individuals.

The fifth chakra of the body

The Throat Chakra is also known as the center for cleansing and the Chakra of truth. It is the first Chakra, or energy center, in the spiritual system. It is the hub of all communication and is also known by the name Vishuddha. The Sound Chakra is related with the mouth, ears, and the thyroid gland in the endocrine system. It is situated along the region of the throat.

Truth, originality, respect, satisfaction, purity, and honor are some of the topics that are discussed. Vishuddha is considered to be in good health in a person who tells the truth and expresses the genuine voice that they possess. But talking shouldn't be the whole focus of this activity. You also need to be an active listener. Communication is a process that goes in both directions. You still need to make the effort to listen, even if you are the one speaking or have something to contribute to the conversation.

Lies, both the kind we tell other people and the kind we tell ourselves, may obstruct the proper flow of energy via the Throat Chakra. A blocked Throat Chakra may present itself in many different ways, including telling white lies. When it comes to your true essence, you can never lie. Who you are cannot be changed. You have to figure out how to make peace with it. In order to assist in opening the Chakra, you will need to let go of your denial and the falsehoods that you tell yourself.

Anger, despair, frustration, grief, pride, poor learning capacity, communication failure, being misunderstood, and the inability to express oneself or get the message out are all symptoms of a blocked Throat Chakra. Other symptoms include an inability to get the message out or express oneself.

When a person's ideas and words are clear, it is easier to understand what they are saying. A lack of comprehension often results in wrath, which is sufficient justification for you to work towards maintaining a healthy Throat Chakra. A lisp, hearing issues, speech disorders, and thyroid problems are all examples of the physical symptoms that might result from a blocked Vishuddha.

During your meditation, picture a blue light so that you may have a clean throat chakra. Allow that light to permeate your whole being, traveling through your body and reaching every crevice. The sound of the vowel is "AI," just as it is in the word "Hi," and some of the affirmations are as follows: "I am open, clear, and honest in my communication." I am aware of when it is appropriate to listen. I am nice and straightforward in my communication.

Simple exercises focusing on the neck will be beneficial for this Chakra. Both the fish posture and the plow pose in yoga focus on the back of the neck and may assist in opening the chakras. Asanas, JalandharaBandhas, and shoulder stands are all examples of yoga positions that may be put into practice. You might also rub some essential oils over your neck, such as sandalwood or lavender. Maintaining a healthy Throat Chakra may also be accomplished by singing, chanting, reading aloud, reciting poetry, playing music, laughing, yelling, or engaging in any other kind of vocalization.

Healing of the Throat Chakra

If you wish to be able to speak and express yourself better, you should look into the several ways that your throat chakra may be healed, which are explained in the following paragraphs.

Remedy via sound

This is the important key to unleashing the energy that is stored in your throat chakra. You should play sound to yourself and let it out. Practice mantras on a regular basis, sing or listen to your favorite tunes, or even chant mantras. Because reflex points on the roof of the mouth convey impulses to the brain, which in turn stimulate certain places in the body, a mantra is a particular sound that, when repeated, vibrates through the nerve system to have a direct influence on the specific chakra.

Increase the amount of natural fluids you consume.

The greatest way to enhance your throat chakra and restore balance in it is to drink fluids that are high in nutritional content. Take in some fresh juices and herbal teas every now and then. Your throat chakra may also be healed by eating certain fruits, notably figs, specifically.

The Ajna Chakra, also known as the Third Eye or Brow Chakra

This is the fifth chakra, and it is placed in the middle of the forehead. It resonates with the color pink, and it is associated with a heavenly insight, an inner vision, intellect, and wisdom. Intuition is also associated with this chakra. Our capacity to concentrate on the bigger picture and our level of awareness are inextricably linked to one another. It is represented as a descending triangle inside a circle, and the diamond is its precious stone. This chakra is personified by the sun, and the spiral that corresponds to it is known as the sacral chakra. It is represented by the sixth sense in our language.

If you are able to picture things via your third eye and have a high degree of intuition as well as a direct spiritual vision, this indicates that your third eye chakra is open and functioning properly. When your third eye chakra isn't functioning properly, you become dogmatic in your thinking and too dependent on the truth of your views. You may have a propensity to put your trust in those in authority, and you may not be very adept at thinking on your own. If you have an overactive third eye chakra, you may find yourself living in a dream world and experience hallucinations.

Eyestrain, headaches, blindness, and impaired vision are some of the physical symptoms that may occur when there are issues with the third eye chakra. The eyes, face, brain, and lymphatic and endocrine systems are the elements of the body that are related with the brow, often known as the third eye. In general, the third eye chakra is the core of psychic ability, higher intuition, and the energies of the spirit and light. This is the reason why the third eye chakra is associated with the element of light. With the help of its abilities, the system rids you of negativity as well as inclinations toward self-centeredness, provides advice, and connects you with your higher self.

Healing of the Third Eye Chakra

In your mind's eye

Since our third eye serves as the starting point for all of our dreams and visions, visualizations are the most effective technique. Our perceptions are twisted and reshaped in the third eye. Through the use of this method, the third eye may be properly repaired.

Consume meals that range from red to violet in hue.

Consuming foods with a purple hue, such as purple potatoes, blackberries, plums, and purple grapes, is an effective way to promote the healing of your third eye chakra. Your brow chakra may also be healed with the consumption of chocolate and spices or drinks scented with lavender.

Yoga Perform child positions as well as other postures that include forward bends in your yoga practice. Enhancing the energy of your third eye chakra may also be accomplished via the practice of eye exercises. After doing these exercises, you may find that applying a soothing herbal oil helps.

Bringing Our Life Force Into Harmony And Purification

The throat chakra, also known as the Vishuddhi chakra, is located close to the larynx. It is the center that assists us in cleansing not just our bodies but also our thoughts and feelings. The poisons in our bodies are cleansed by the throat chakra, which contributes to our overall wellness. Our capacity to 'think before speaking' is improved, and we acquire the ability to communicate more clearly as a result. We hone the nuanced skill of using words tactfully in order to protect the feelings of others.

One of the most admirable qualities of human beings is their capacity for introspection. The practice of meditation gives us the opportunity to reflect on our actions of the past and prompts us to question the caliber of our ideas, behaviors, and feelings. On the one hand, we want for love and relationships that are honest and open with one another. On the other hand, our anxieties and complexes are a constant presence in our lives and hinder us from being honest with ourselves.

We have come to the conclusion that we are the sum total of our positive and negative ideas, feelings, and actions. In the same way that we have been harmed by the malicious words said by other people, we have also been victims of our own wrath and grief, and we have taken it out on other people. We are aware that, in some way, shape, or form, we contributed in some way to the issue at hand, and we know that placing blame on others will not relieve us of the burden of guilt that accompanies us.

Nevertheless, the core of each positive and negative experience propels us forward along the road of spiritual, emotional, and mental development. Each new adventure forces us to expand our horizons and brings us closer to adulthood. We are able to learn to center our attention on the genuine significance of our life so that we are not swept away by the sway of our ideas and feelings. We are aware that we have been given a tremendous amount of potential blessings. All that is required of us is to tap into it and channel it so that we may live lives that have greater significance.

We will, for the first time, start to accept the truth about ourselves, which is that we were the obstacles in the way of our own advancement on the road toward improvement. We begin to cultivate the virtue of patience and begin to direct our attention toward developing our own unique abilities. This chakra is connected to artistic endeavors that are in some way linked to the vocal chords, such as teaching, writing, singing, and composing poetry.

Practices That Are Useful Sitting in silence for a period of time on a regular basis is a very straightforward and efficient method that trains us to think before we speak. We acquire the ability to choose our words carefully.

We are more able to connect with our authentic selves when we chant the mantra HAM. This mantra guides us through the process of being more self-aware and assists us in developing our full potential.

The most effective method for cleansing and restoring the chakra's equilibrium is to practice pranayama, which consists of breathing exercises.

This chakra is represented by the color blue, which is also its related color. This chakra may be activated, cleansed, and calmed with the use of crystals like as aquamarine, apatite, turquoise, and blue tiger eye.

In the course of our meditation sessions, we gain clarity as we concentrate on the part that we play in each circumstance. It's possible that we've caused harm to other people without even recognizing it, and what's more significant is that we could have caused harm to ourselves by burying the anguish and suffering that was created by other people. We are taught to communicate in a kind and diplomatic manner. The other person is given the ability to think independently as a result of this empowerment. We acquire the ability to articulate our perspectives, feelings, and ideas in a straightforward and uncomplicated manner.

The jalandharibandha, ujjayipranayam, matsyasana, sarvangasana, and shirsasana, setuasana, and other yoga postures are some of the breathing and stretching activities that are associated with the throat chakra.

Bringing the Chakra Points to a Close

Before you bring yourself out of a meditative state, it is important to make sure that your chakras are closed. If you do not block your chakras, you will make yourself vulnerable to having the energy from individuals around you, who do not have control over their own energy fields, drawn into your body and used by them.

You should leave them slightly open to enable the continuing of energy to flow unrestrained, but you should make sure to shut the tap sufficiently that it leaves just a steady trickle running until you become skilled at regulating your energy. Leaving them slightly open will allow the continuation of energy to flow unrestricted.

The act of closing your Chakras is analogous to doing the opposite of expanding them. You should begin at the Crown and work your way down to the Root. When shutting, the hue should be toned down rather than brightened.

When shutting, do not entirely shut down the Chakras; rather, you should ensure that a little amount of energy is still steadily moving through each of them. While you are reducing the brightness of the color, go to the next Chakra before you have entirely reduced the brightness of the previous Chakra, leaving it with a dull glow.

Once you feel that you have properly closed down, rest for a few minutes as you gently return your breathing rate to normal.

www.ingramcontent.com/pod-product-compliance
Lightning Source LLC
Chambersburg PA
CBHW052135110526
44591CB00012B/1724